LEOPARDS

A TRUE BOOK®

by
Ann O. Squire

Children's Press®
A Division of Scholastic Inc.

New York Toronto London Auckland Sydney
Mexico City New Delhi Hong Kong
Danbury, Connecticut

A leopard
mother and cub

Reading Consultant
Nanci R. Vargus, Ed.D.
*Assistant Professor, School
of Education, University of
Indianapolis*

Content Consultant
Kathy Carlstead, Ph.D.
*Research Scientist,
Honolulu Zoo*

Dedication:
For Emma

Library of Congress Cataloging-in-Publication Data

Squire, Ann.O.
    Leopards / by Ann O. Squire.
        p. cm. — (A true book)
Includes bibliographical references and index.
    ISBN 0-516-22794-7 (lib. bdg.)   0-516-27934-3 (pbk.)
    1. Leopard—Juvenile literature. I. Title. II. Series.
QL737.C23S6398 2004
599.75'54—dc22

                                                2004007755

1 2 3 4 5 6 7 8 9 10 R 14 13 12 11 10 09 08 07 06 05

Contents

A leopard in a tree

Cat Up a Tree

If you went on a safari to Africa, you'd expect to see many amazing sights. You might see a thundering herd of wildebeest, or a sleek cheetah streaking across the dry grassland. There's one thing you'd never expect to see, however: a full-grown antelope draped over a tree branch 20 feet (6 meters) above the ground. What on Earth is an antelope doing in a tree? How did it get there?

If you look closely, you'll see that the antelope is dead, maybe even half-eaten. It was dragged up the tree by a leopard, one of the strongest and most skillful hunters on the African plains.

Besides being one of the strongest wild cats, the leopard

This leopard has dragged an antelope into a tree to keep it away from other predators.

is also one of the hardest to spot. In fact, you are much more likely to see the remains of a leopard's meal than the leopard itself. Many visitors to Africa leave without ever having seen this **elusive** spotted cat.

Because leopards are so rarely seen by humans, many people think that they are very rare. In fact, leopards are found in more places, and in more different **habitats,** than any other wild cat. Besides Africa, leopards live in many parts of southern Asia and the Middle East. They live in forests, grasslands, mountains, woodlands, and many other

Leopards can be found in a variety of habitats, including forests, deserts, and snowy mountainous regions.

habitats. They eat almost anything, from insects, rodents, and small mammals to impala, gazelle, and even young giraffes.

All leopards have black spots arranged in a ring or "rosette" pattern. The background color of the coat differs, however, depending on where the leopard lives. In general, leopards that live in open grasslands have golden yellow coats, those

A close-up view of the "rosette" pattern on a leopard's coat

Leopards that live on grasslands (left) tend to have lighter coats than those that live deep in the forest (above).

that live in rain forests have dark gold coats, and those living in the mountains are darker still. Sometimes, an all-black leopard will be born in a litter of normal-colored cubs. These black leopards, also called black panthers, are most often found in the dark rain forests of India and Southeast Asia.

A black leopard

A Skillful Hunter

Leopards are among the most skillful hunters in the cat family. They **stalk** their **prey** mainly at night, using the cover of darkness to creep close to their unknowing victims. Their sharp eyesight allows them to see in the dark. Their extra-long whiskers help

Leopards have excellent vision and long whiskers that help them find their way while hunting in the dark.

them feel their way through thick **underbrush.**

Compared to other wild cats such as lions and tigers, leopards are somewhat small. An adult male weighs only 130 pounds (59 kilograms), about one-third as much as an adult lion. Leopards must compete not only with lions, but also with hyenas and jackals that try to steal their food. To avoid these competitors, leopards often drag prey animals high into the trees.

A hyena crouching over
a kill that it has stolen
from two leopards

A leopard dragging away an antelope it has just killed

As you can imagine, leopards are incredibly strong. They have been seen hauling young giraffes up to the treetops. This is an amazing feat, considering that these animals weigh two or three times as much as a leopard.

How does the leopard do it?
The muscles in this cat's chest
and shoulders are extremely
large, so the leopard is able to
pull heavy loads. The leopard also
has a huge head; powerful jaw
muscles; and long, sharp canine
teeth that it uses to grip its prey.

This yawning leopard is showing off its powerful jaws.

Little Leopards

Like most other big cats, leopards live and hunt alone. They set up **territories** where other leopards are not welcome. To claim ownership of a territory, a leopard marks rocks and trees with a smelly spray of urine or makes scratches on a tree trunk.

Leopards are solitary animals. This means that they live and hunt alone.

Female leopards stake out territories that range in size from 4 to 12 square miles (10 to 31 square kilometers). No other females are allowed inside another female's territory. Male leopards have territories that are larger and that **overlap** several female territories.

Most of the time, male and female leopards ignore each other. Occasionally, however, they get together for mating. After spending several days

A male and female leopard together at mating time

A female
leopard
nursing
her cubs

together, the male and female split up.

In about three months, the female gives birth to a litter of two or three tiny, helpless cubs. For the first few months of their lives, the cubs stay in hiding while their mother goes out to hunt.

When they are about three months old, they are ready to start following her. The mother leopard leads the way as she moves through the underbrush in search of prey. She holds her long tail straight up, so that the furry white tip can be seen above the tall grasses. By keeping an eye on their mother's tail, the cubs are able to follow along without getting lost.

Leopard cubs stay with their mother for nearly two years. During this time, she teaches them everything they will need to know to survive in the wild. After two years have

A leopard and her cub stalk a herd of wildebeest.

passed, the cubs are ready to leave their mother and find territories of their own.

A Trio of Leopards

Besides the familiar African leopard, there are two other species of big cats that are called "leopards." The clouded leopard lives in the rain forests of Southeast Asia. The snow leopard lives in the high mountains of central Asia. Many people assume that these cats

Clouded leopards are found in the Asian countries of China, Nepal, Thailand, Indonesia, and Borneo.

are **varieties** of the leopard found in Africa, but this is not true. Each is a completely different **species.** However, just like the African leopard, both of these species are perfectly **adapted** to the environments in which they live.

Some Teeth!

Most mammals have long, pointed teeth on either side of their front teeth. These teeth, called canines, are used for grabbing and tearing food. For its size, the clouded leopard has the longest canine teeth of any cat.

The clouded leopard gets its name from the uneven markings on its coat. Some people think that the large, black-edged spots look like clouds. Clouded leopards are much smaller than African leopards and are even better tree climbers. Some people have seen clouded leopards run down tree trunks head first, or hang upside down from branches by their hind feet.

Clouded leopards spend a lot of time in the treetops. They

A clouded leopard in a tree waits for prey to walk below.

wait on overhanging branches for prey on the ground to walk below them, and then spring upon them. Their prey includes birds, small mammals, and monkeys.

The snow leopard is perfectly suited to its cold, snowy, mountainous surroundings. It has long, dense fur and an extra-long tail. A snow leopard

The snow leopard has an incredibly long tail.

may wrap this fluffy tail around its face, using it almost like a warm scarf.

The snow leopard also has large paws covered by a thick cushion of fur. In addition to keeping the cat's feet warm, the fur increases the area of the foot in contact with the ground. This turns the leopard's paws into snowshoes, so that the cat is able to walk on top of the snow instead of sinking in.

Snow leopards have wide, furry paws that act almost like snowshoes.

A snow leopard
leaping toward prey

Like other cats, snow leopards stalk and pounce on their prey. These cats are champion jumpers, and they are able to leap on prey animals up to 45 feet (14 m) away!

The Right Kind of Nose

The nasal passages of the snow leopard are bigger than those of other leopard species. Since they live high in the mountains, where the air is thinner, it may be that this adaptation helps snow leopards get enough oxygen.

Leopards in Danger

It's true that leopards are adaptable and are found in lots of different habitats. Like other big cats, however, leopards face many threats. Whether they live in Africa, China, Thailand, or Tibet, leopards are in danger. Forests are being cut down and more and more land is being

In both Africa (above) and Asia, leopards are losing their habitats as forests are cut down to make way for farmland.

used for farming and ranching. Leopards have fewer places to live and have more trouble finding their natural prey.

When this happens, they sometimes attack livestock or even people. The farmers respond by poisoning, trapping, or shooting the leopards.

Another threat to all leopard species is poaching, or illegal hunting. Even though leopards are protected by law, there are still people who kill them. They sell their beautiful spotted coats, their teeth, and even their bones, which are used in traditional Asian medicine.

Police in India seizing skins of illegally hunted leopards and tigers

An African leopard
and her cubs

What can you do to help? Learn all you can about leopards by reading books and visiting your local zoo. Raise money and contribute to organizations that help wild cats. Let your parents and other adults know how important it is to protect leopards and other wild cat species. It is up to all of us to make sure these beautiful cats have a place on Earth for years to come.

To Find Out More

Here are some additional resources to help you learn more about leopards:

 **Books**

Feeney, Kathy. **Leopards** (Our Wild World). Northward Press, 2002.

Klevansk, Rhonda. **Big Cats.** Lorenz, 1999.

Markle, Sandra. **Outside and Inside Big Cats.** Atheneum, 2003.

Saign, Geoffrey C. **The African Cats.** Franklin Watts, 1999.

Vogel, Elizabeth. **Leopards** (Big Cats). Rosen Publishing Group, 2002.

Organizations and Online Sites

The Clouded Leopard Project
http://www.clouded leopard.org

The Web site of his conservation organization includes information on clouded leopards, threats to their survival, and efforts to save them.

Cyber Zoomobile
http://www.home.global crossing.net/~brendel/

The Cyber Zoomobile Web site has pictures and information on African leopards, clouded leopards, and snow leopards, as well as other cat species.

International Snow Leopard Trust
http://www.snowleopard.org

The Web site of the International Snow Leopard Trust offers information on snow leopards and efforts to save these cats in the wild.

Important Words

adapted when a living thing has developed physical features that help it fit in better with its environment

elusive very hard to find

habitats places where animals or plants naturally live and grow

overlap to cover part of something

prey animal hunted by other animals

species group of animals whose members can mate and have offspring

stalk to creep up slowly and quietly on a prey animal

territories areas that animals live in and defend

underbrush bushes, shrubs, and other plants that grow beneath large trees

varieties different types of the same thing

Index

Meet the Author

Ann O. Squire has a Ph.D. in animal behavior. Before becoming a writer, she spent several years studying African electric fish and the special signals they use to communicate with each other. Dr. Squire is the author of many books on animals and natural science topics, including *Jaguars, Tigers, African Animals*, and *Animal Homes*. She and her children, Emma and Evan, share their home with a not-so-wild cat named Isabel.